INSIDER'S LOOK

D1026459

LIFE INSIDE THE NAVAL ACADEMY

JIL FINE

HIGH
interest
books

Children's Press®
A Division of Scholastic Inc.
New York/Toronto/London/Auckland/Sydney
Mexico City/New Delhi/Hong Kong
Danbury, Connecticut

Book Design: Daniel Hosek
Contributing Editor: Eric Fein

Special thanks to Kirk Schneider, David Radford, Jiordan DiOrio, and Jason Mattila

Photo Credits: Cover © Paul A. Souders/Corbis; p. 5 Michael S. Yamashita/Corbis;
p. 6 © Corbis; pp. 9, 32, 35 © Lowell Georgia/Corbis; pp. 10, 22, 27, 34, 41 courtesy of
Defense Visual Information Center, March ARB, California; pp. 11, 14, 21, 24, 29, 31
© Anna Clopet/Corbis; p. 12 © Reuters NewMedia Inc./Corbis; p. 17 © Bob Rowan/
Progressive Image/Corbis; p. 19 © Duomo/Corbis; p. 23 © Kevin Fleming/Corbis;
p. 27 © Robert Maass/Corbis; p. 37 © Aero Graphics/Corbis; p. 39 © Douglas
Peebles/Corbis; p. 40 © Annie Griffiths Belt/Corbis

Library of Congress Cataloging-in-Publication Data

Fine, Jil.
Life inside the Naval Academy / Jil Fine.
    p. cm. -- (Insider's look)
Includes index.
Summary: Explores the challenges and rewards of attending the Naval
Academy in Annapolis, Maryland, where individuals are trained to become
officers in the United States Navy or Marine Corps.
ISBN 0-516-23922-8 (library binding) -- ISBN 0-516-24005-6 (pbk.)
1. United States Naval Academy--Juvenile literature. [1. United States
Naval Academy. 2. Occupations.] I. Title. II. Series.
V415.P1 F55 2002
359'.0071'173--dc21

                                                           2002001899

CONTENTS

Introduction

In times of international crisis, the United States turns to the men and women of its armed services for protection. Skilled officers must be ready for action at all times. Some officers rise through the ranks of the military. Others go to schools or academies that specialize in training America's future military leaders.

The U.S. Navy and U.S. Marine Corps rely on the Naval Academy in Annapolis, Maryland, to train their officers. The U.S. Navy pays for tuition, room, board, and medical and dental insurance coverage of students who attend the academy. In return, midshipmen, or students, must agree to serve in the

Graduates of the U.S. Naval Academy serve on warships all over the world.

For Naval Academy graduates, the stars are the limit!

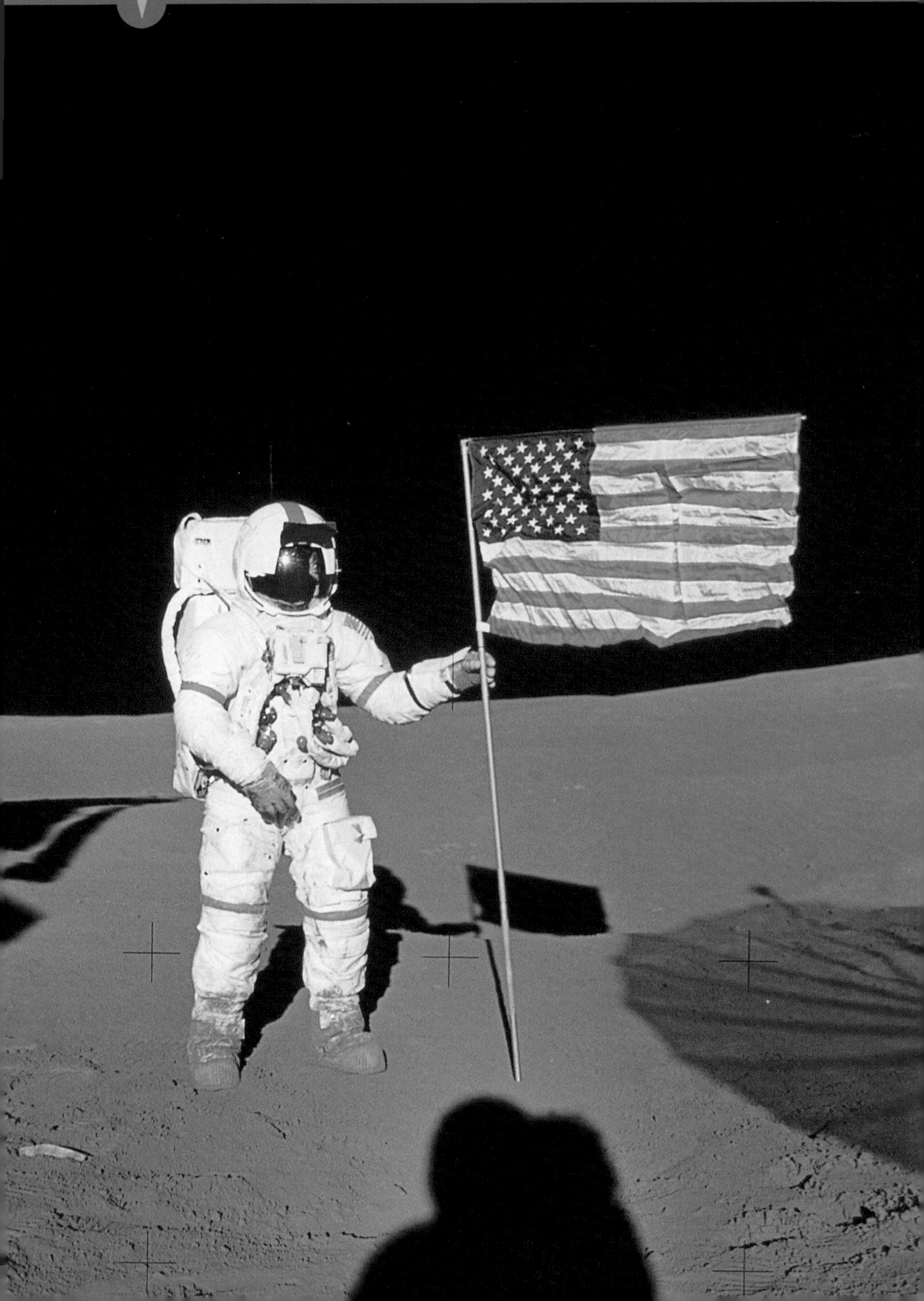

U.S. Navy or U.S. Marine Corps for a total of twelve years. This includes four years of schooling at the Naval Academy, five years of active duty afterward, and three years of reserve duty.

Midshipmen at the Naval Academy have very different experiences from young people who go to civilian colleges. Have you ever wondered what life is like at the Naval Academy? Or what it takes to get in? This book will give you an inside look. You'll learn that life in the Naval Academy can be exciting, challenging—and busy. A midshipman's day is filled with military training, drills, exercise, and classes. He or she learns about military history, military life, and how officers are expected to act.

Naval Academy graduates have many career opportunities. After four years in the Naval Academy, graduates are ready to become officers in the U.S. Navy or the U.S. Marines. There is no limit to what a Naval Academy graduate may achieve. Fifty-four Naval Academy graduates have become National Aeronautic and Space Administration (NASA) astronauts! Life inside the Naval Academy is a unique challenge. Let's take a closer look at what it's all about.

CHAPTER ONE

A Few Good Midshipmen

The Naval Academy has been training young people to become U.S. Navy and U.S. Marine officers for more than 150 years. The Naval Academy started in 1845. At that time, it was called the Naval School. George Bancroft, Secretary of the U.S. Navy, started the school to train naval officers. Secretary Bancroft chose 10 acres of land in Annapolis, Maryland, for the location of the school. The Naval School opened its doors on October 10, 1845. About fifty midshipmen were in the first class. Each midshipman spent five years at the Naval School. During the first and fifth years, they attended classes. The three middle years were spent training at sea.

The U.S. Naval Academy is located in Annapolis, Maryland, near the banks of the Severn River.

In 1850, the Naval School's name was changed to the Naval Academy. The program was shortened to four years of combined military training and education. Training at sea was performed during the summers. This program is similar to the one in use today. The Naval Academy has grown a lot since 1845. The site at Annapolis now occupies 338 acres of land. Each year, about 4,000 men and women attend the Naval Academy.

MISSION: POSSIBLE

The Naval Academy's mission is to develop military leaders who are morally, physically, and mentally fit and prepared for action. Midshipmen have rigid physical and academic requirements to meet. They must pass exams as well as physical fitness tests each semester. Midshipmen are also expected to be truthful and honorable in all that they do or say. If they are found to have lied, cheated, or

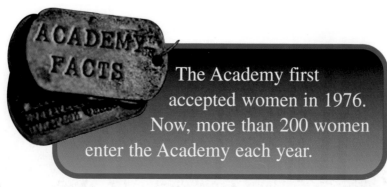

ACADEMY FACTS

The Academy first accepted women in 1976. Now, more than 200 women enter the Academy each year.

Midshipmen at the Naval Academy are always ready for action!

San Antonio Spur David Robinson learned to stand tall during his time at the Naval Academy.

stolen, they can be kicked out of the academy. The standards are high for the Naval Academy's midshipmen. Even so, most students meet the challenge. About 77 percent of the men and women who enter the Naval Academy complete the program and graduate.

Many graduates of the Naval Academy have gone on to do big things. Jimmy Carter, former president of the United States, was trained at the Naval Academy. Alan Shepard Jr. graduated from the Naval Academy in 1944. He was the first American astronaut in space. Another famous Naval Academy graduate is David Robinson. Robinson played basketball while going to the Naval Academy. Now, he starts for the San Antonio Spurs in the National Basketball Association.

WHAT DOES IT TAKE?

Midshipmen come from all over the United States and from U.S. territories, such as Puerto Rico and Guam. Each year, about 10,000 students apply for admission to the Naval Academy. Only about 1,100 are accepted.

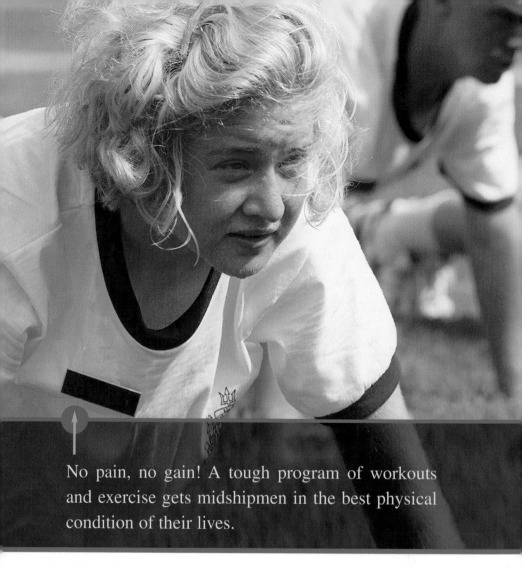

No pain, no gain! A tough program of workouts and exercise gets midshipmen in the best physical condition of their lives.

Basic requirements for admission to the Naval Academy are unlike those of civilian colleges. Applicants must be U.S. citizens between the ages of 17 and 23. They cannot be married, pregnant, or a parent.

Anyone seeking admission must pass medical, dental, and physical fitness tests. The physical fitness test is called the Physical Aptitude Examination. It consists of a 300-yard run, a kneeling basketball throw, a standing long jump, and pull-ups (or a flexed-arm hang for women). If you are overweight on the first day of classes, you may be turned away, even if you already passed the fitness test! The tough physical requirements for admission to the Naval Academy ensure that you can handle the difficult training to come in the next four years.

Most colleges ask for a letter of reference from a teacher or school counselor when you apply. The Naval Academy asks for a nomination, or appointment, from a U.S. senator, representative, or other type of official. Some people even get a nomination from the president! But don't worry, you don't have to know the president or a senator to get a nomination. Each year, officials give a limited number of nominations to high school students who want to attend the Naval Academy. The Naval Academy admission office has a list of officials whom you may contact for a nomination.

They also have sample letters that many students use to request a nomination. The application process for the Naval Academy takes more time than the process at other colleges. It's recommended that students interested in attending the academy should start applying in their junior year of high school.

There are several ways to improve your chances of getting into the Naval Academy. Getting good grades is an important way to get noticed. The classes you take in high school are also important. Four years of English and mathematics are strongly recommended. Take algebra, geometry, and trigonometry for your math classes. Two years of a foreign language and at least one year of chemistry, physics, U.S. history, and European or world history will also help your chances of getting accepted. Having good computer skills and participating in a variety of after-school activities are very important. Participation in after-school activities shows that you can manage your time well. In 2001, most people admitted to the Naval Academy participated in an after-school activity, such as varsity athletics or theater.

Earning good grades by working hard in high school will improve your chances of getting into the Naval Academy.

If you are interested in going to the Naval Academy, you can visit the school to get a first-hand look at campus life. The Naval Academy has a special summer seminar for high school students, between their junior and senior years. There is a lot of competition to get into the summer seminar. Most of the students who are accepted to the seminar have a grade point average of 3.5 or higher. They are in the top 20 percent of their class and have already taken the SATs.

About 1,100 high school students from around the world attend the summer seminar each year. The seminar lasts six days. The demanding schedule gives high school students a taste of Naval Academy life. During the summer seminar, students wake up at 6:30 A.M. with the blowing of reveille. Reveille is a wake-up call played on a bugle. It serves as an alarm clock for all midshipmen. Morning exercise begins the day and is followed by attending workshops on literature, history, sailing, or physics. Later in the day, there is time for military drills or sports. Students are introduced to the kind of athletic and military training that they would receive if they became midshipmen in the Naval Academy. The bugle plays taps at 11:00 P.M., signaling the end of the day and lights out.

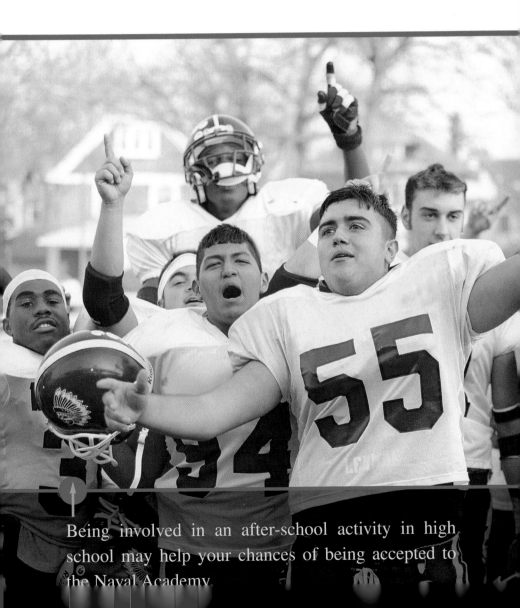

Being involved in an after-school activity in high school may help your chances of being accepted to the Naval Academy.

CHAPTER TWO

Getting Your Sea Legs

Men and women in their first year at the Naval Academy are called plebes. Plebes report to the Naval Academy on July 1. The summer before classes start is called Plebe Summer. The first day of Plebe Summer is called Induction Day. On Induction Day, plebes are given medical tests, a military haircut, and a bag of gear.

Plebes also take the Oath of Office on Induction Day. They must promise to be loyal to their country, and to serve and defend it. Here, they also make the commitment to a military lifestyle for the next twelve years.

Once a student has accepted a spot in the Naval Academy, he or she is a member of the

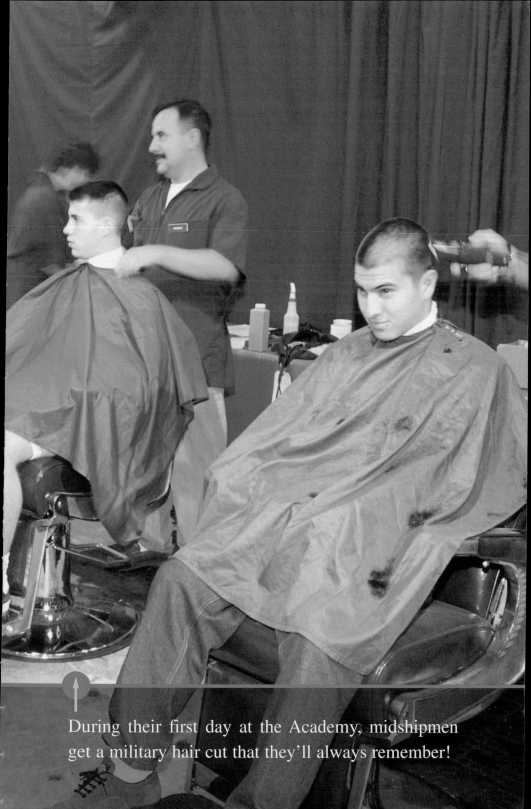

During their first day at the Academy, midshipmen get a military hair cut that they'll always remember!

ACADEMY FACTS

Bancroft Hall is one of the largest dormitories in the United States. It has 1,873 rooms with 5 miles of hallways and 33 acres of floor space. King Hall, the enormous Naval Academy dining room, is inside Bancroft Hall.

armed forces. If the midshipman decides to quit, he or she may still have a duty to serve in the U.S. Navy. The student may also have to pay for supplies and tuition.

Like other midshipmen, plebes eat in King Hall. King Hall has 360 tables, enough to seat all four thousand midshipmen in the Naval Academy. Plebes also begin their stay at Bancroft Hall, the academy's dormitory. All midshipmen live in Bancroft Hall. They lovingly call it "Mother B."

Plebes are taught how to salute, stand at attention, sail and navigate a boat, and more. Time is also spent learning to march correctly, and to keep rooms orderly and uniforms clean.

Life on the Naval Academy campus is challenging—
and highly rewarding.

There's no such thing as taking it easy at the
Naval Academy.

Plebes spend more than 100 hours exercising throughout the summer. Each day, plebes do 75 minutes of exercises like running, push-ups, and sit-ups.

DOWN TIME

Plebes are given only a small amount of time each day for personal activities. They can play sports, attend religious services, or call or write home during this time. Plebes also get matched up with local Annapolis families who act as guides to the city. On Saturdays, plebes can spend time with these families.

NAVAL ACADEMY MAJORS

- Aerospace Engineering
- Chemistry
- Computer Science
- Economics
- Electrical Engineering
- English
- General Engineering
- General Science
- History
- Mathematics
- Mechanical Engineering
- Naval Architecture
- Ocean Engineering
- Oceanography
- Physics
- Political Science
- Quantitative Economics
- Systems Engineering

At the end of Plebe Summer, parents are invited to a three-day event called Parent's Weekend. Plebes show their parents around the "Yard." The Yard is the Naval Academy's campus. Many plebes use this weekend to show their parents all that they have learned over the summer.

PLEBE YEAR

After Plebe Summer ends, plebes settle into Naval Academy life with the other midshipmen. Like a civilian college year, the Naval Academy's year is broken up into fall and spring semesters. A plebe's first year is filled with classes such as calculus, chemistry, and naval science. By the end of the first year, each plebe chooses a major. There are eighteen majors offered by the Naval Academy. Any major that a plebe chooses will prepare him or her for a career in the U.S. Navy or U.S. Marines.

IN THE SWIM OF THINGS

In addition to training during the school year, midshipmen go out to sea each summer. Unlike civilian college students, midshipmen don't get a full summer break. They must attend summer

ACADEMY FACTS

Learning the Honor Concept is an important part of life at the Naval Academy. The Honor Concept states that midshipmen must not lie, cheat, or steal. It also states that midshipmen should always stand for what they believe is right. Brigade Honor Committees of upper class midshipmen keep a watchful eye on other midshipmen to make sure that the Honor Concept is being followed. The upper classmen are also there to set a good example for others. Those who violate, or go against, the Honor Concept can be made to leave the academy.

Midshipmen take the Naval Academy's Honor Concept very seriously.

training for the U.S. Navy or the U.S. Marines. During the summer between the first and second year of school, midshipmen patrol various ports throughout New England. They spend time on a 44-foot sailboat or take part in training operations. The operations are like those practiced by the U.S. Navy SEALS and the U.S. Marines.

In the following summer, midshipmen learn to fly U.S. Navy aircraft, dive in a submarine, and fight against an enemy. They also work as members of a crew on a ship or submarine for four weeks. In their final summer, midshipmen choose a summer activity based on what they would like to do after graduation. Midshipmen can choose to work as junior officers with a real U.S. Navy or U.S. Marine unit.

Nothing floats a midshipman's boat like working at sea.

CHAPTER THREE

On the Go

A DAY IN THE LIFE

A typical day for a midshipman starts with the blowing of reveille at 6:30 A.M. Once awake, the midshipman's day follows a rigid schedule. Room and uniform inspection by higher-ranking midshipmen is first on the schedule. Demerits, or bad marks, are given to those who do not meet the academy's high standards. Breakfast is served in King Hall at 7:10 A.M. Meals are served to the entire brigade, or student body, within just 4 minutes. Mealtime lasts for 45 minutes. Then, it's off to class.

The first four classes of the day are each 1 hour long. Classes at the Naval Academy are

At the Naval Academy, midshipmen learn about navigation using the latest high-tech equipment.

Men and women stand shoulder to shoulder, working
their way through the Naval Academy.

small, with fewer than twenty-two midshipmen in each class. At 12:05 P.M., all midshipmen gather in front of Bancroft Hall. They march together to lunch. The midshipmen enter King Hall at 12:15 P.M. At 12:40 P.M., each midshipman goes to join his or her company for training time.

There are thirty companies in the entire Naval Academy brigade. Each company eats, sleeps, drills, studies, and plays together. Companies compete for the title of Color Company by getting points for academic, professional, and athletic excellence. Any individual demerits received for untidy rooms or uniforms affect an entire company's chances of earning the title. The company that earns this title gets special privileges for the following year. One privilege includes representing the Naval Academy at official functions, such as the presidential inauguration.

Training time ends at 1:20 P.M. The fifth class begins at 1:30 P.M. After the sixth class ends at 3:30 P.M., it's time for sports or other activities. From 3:30 P.M. to 6:00 P.M., midshipmen can choose to play football, work on a play, sing, or do many other activities.

Supper is served from 5:00 P.M. to 7:00 P.M. After supper, it is time to study and do homework. The study period for all midshipmen is from 7:30 P.M. to 11:00 P.M. At 11:00 P.M., it's lights out for plebes. Upper class midshipmen get to stay up for an extra hour. Almost every single minute of the students' day is scheduled. It is up to each midshipman to get his or her work done in the time allowed.

TIME OFF AND A PAYCHECK

Leave, or time off, is given to midshipmen as a reward for good behavior. All midshipmen are given leave for Thanksgiving and Christmas. They also get leave midway through each spring semester and for a week at the end of the spring semester. Midshipmen are given a total of thirty days leave in the summer.

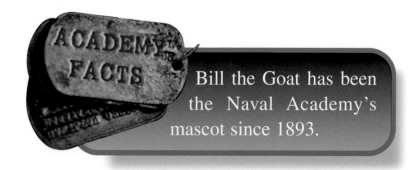

ACADEMY FACTS Bill the Goat has been the Naval Academy's mascot since 1893.

Midshipmen are paid for their service at the Naval Academy. The monthly pay is $699. However, fees for services, such as haircuts, shoe repair, and laundry, are deducted. Fees for supplies and uniforms are also deducted. Out of the $699, plebes are usually left with about $100 in spending money each month. Every year, the amount received increases until senior year, when the firsties, or seniors, receive about $300 a month in spending money.

The academy's mascot, Bill the Goat, is a fan favorite when he takes the field at Navy football games.

CHAPTER FOUR

Ready for Action!

After four years of study and hard work at the Naval Academy, midshipmen are ready to become military officers. Upon graduating from the Naval Academy, at least five years of active service are required from each graduate. Active service means that you are working for the U.S. Navy or U.S. Marines. If a graduate decides to go into aviation, the required time for service may be eight or nine years. No matter what job a graduate chooses, he or she will probably lead men and women who have enlisted, or signed up without training, in the U.S. Navy or U.S. Marines.

The most popular choice for graduates is to become a U.S. Navy pilot. Pilots may fly helicopters, patrol planes, or fighter jets. In 2000, 235 Naval Academy graduates chose to become pilots. Some graduates choose to work behind the scenes in the radar and air traffic control departments.

Many graduates also choose surface warfare. Surface warfare officers are stationed on aircraft carriers or battleships. Graduates can choose the type of ship that they want to work on. They can also choose the home port, or location, of their first assignment. These assignments last for about two years. Officers train to find enemy submarines and get experience with weapons and communications.

Want to be a top gun? Some Naval Academy graduates go on to get their wings as U.S. Navy pilots.

Working on submarines is another choice for Naval Academy graduates. They can choose to work with weapons, engineering, communications, or even nuclear power on submarines. A submarine tour of duty, or assignment, is three years long.

There is also the field of special operations and special warfare. The men and women who enter this field perform diving and other work to find mines and dangerous explosives. The famous U.S. Navy SEALS are a branch of the U.S. Special Operations Forces.

Some academy graduates choose to go into the U.S. Marine Corps. U.S. Marines may be assigned anywhere in the world. They may work with ground or air forces. Many graduates are assigned positions to lead thirty-five to forty-three enlisted U.S. Marines.

Women can choose almost any of the above jobs. However, they are not allowed to serve on submarines or in the U.S. Navy SEALS. In the Marine Corps, women are not allowed to serve in infantry, artillery, or armor units.

About 90 percent of the class of 2001 got their first choice assignments. The average tour of

Many academy grads choose to work aboard the immense aircraft carriers of the U.S. Navy.

Hats off to the graduates! After four years of hard work, Naval Academy graduates have a great reason to celebrate.

duty is about two years long. During this time, young officers discover their strengths and weaknesses, along with their likes and dislikes. After the first tour of duty, some graduates decide to change their career path.

There are many differences between the Naval Academy and a civilian college or university. The strict military lifestyle of the Naval Academy requires a special kind of dedication and hard work. The decision to enter the Naval Academy is a big one. It will change your life forever. In four years, you become a trained soldier and sailor. Attending the Naval Academy can be a rewarding experience for the right person.

ACADEMY FACTS

Graduation is a big day for midshipmen. The U.S. president or vice president speaks at the graduation ceremony each year. Also, the U.S. Navy's famous team of jet fighters, the Blue Angels, performs stunts to celebrate the graduates' achievements.

NEW WORDS

application a form that is used for acceptance to college

brigade the entire student body of the Naval Academy

bugle a musical instrument shaped like a trumpet but without keys

civilian someone who is not a member of the armed forces

demerit a mark against someone, usually for doing something wrong

drill a training exercise; to teach people a skill by having them repeat it over and over again

honor keeping promises and behaving in a way that earns respect from others

Induction Day the plebes' first day at the Naval Academy, usually July 1

NEW WORDS

midshipmen Naval Academy students

officer someone who is in charge of other people and is in a position of responsibility in the armed forces

plebe a first year midshipman

reference a written statement about someone's character or abilities

requirement something that you need to do or have

reveille a piece of music used as a morning wake-up call in the military

seminar a meeting or class where information is shared

taps a bugle call played at the end of the day in military camps or schools as a signal that all lights must be turned off

FOR FURTHER READING

Abramovitz, Melissa. *The U.S. Navy at War*. Mankato, MN: Capstone Press, 2001.

Bledsoe, Glen, and Karen Bledsoe. *The Blue Angels: The U.S. Navy Flight Demonstration Squadron*. Mankato, MN: Capstone Press, 2001.

Frost, Helen. *The United States Navy*. Mankato, MN: Capstone Press, 1998.

Gaines, Ann Graham. *The Navy in Action*. Berkeley Heights, NJ: Enslow Publishers, 2001.

Naden, Corinne J., and Rose Blue. *The U.S. Navy*. Brookfield, CT: Millbrook Press, 1994.

Streissguth, Tom. *U.S. Navy SEALS*. Mankato, MN: Capstone Press, 1995.

Van Orden, M. D. *U.S. Navy Ships and Coast Guard Cutters*. Annapolis, MD: Naval Institute Press, 2000.

RESOURCES

ORGANIZATIONS

CANDIDATE GUIDANCE OFFICE

United States Naval Academy
117 Decatur Road
Annapolis, MD 21402-5018
(410) 293-4361

UNITED STATES NAVAL SEA CADETS CORPS

2300 Wilson Boulevard
Arlington, VA 22201-3308
(703) 243-6910
www.seacadets.org

RESOURCES

WEB SITES

THE UNITED STATES NAVAL ACADEMY'S OFFICIAL WEB SITE

www.usna.edu

This Web site has a lot of information about life in the Naval Academy and instructions on how to apply.

THE UNITED STATES NAVY'S OFFICIAL WEB SITE

www.navy.mil

This official Web site has inside information about U.S. Navy careers.

THE UNITED STATES MARINES' OFFICIAL WEB SITE

www.marines.com

Find out about the many different careers and opportunities available in the U.S. Marines on the official Web site.

INDEX

INDEX

ABOUT THE AUTHOR

Jil Fine is a freelance writer living in New York City.
Annapolis, Maryland, is her hometown.